FALLING AWAKE

FALLING AWAKE

Alice Oswald

CAPE POETRY

Published by Jonathan Cape 2016

2 4 6 8 10 9 7 5 3 1

First published in Great Britain in 2016 by Jonathan Cape
20 Vauxhall Bridge Road, London SW1V 2SA
www.vintage-books.co.uk

A Penguin Random House Company

Penguin
Random House
UK

global.penguinrandomhouse.com

A CIP catalogue record for this book is available from the British Library

ISBN 9781910702437
Limited edition ISBN 9781910702444

Penguin Random House is committed to a sustainable future for
our business, our readers and our planet. This book is made from
Forest Stewardship Council® certified paper

Typeset for Alice Oswald by Kevin Mount
Printed and bound in Great Britain by TJ International Ltd, Padstow, Cornwall

CONTENTS

A Short Story of Falling   1

Swan   2

Flies   4

Fox   5

Severed Head Floating Downriver   6

Cold Streak   11

Body   12

A Rushed Account of the Dew   13

Shadow   14

Village   17

Vertigo   22

Looking Down   24

Alongside Beans   26

A Drink from Cranmere Pool   28

Slowed-Down Blackbird   29

Dunt   31

Two Voices   36

Sunday Ballad   37

You Must Never Sleep under a Magnolia   38

Aside   39

Sz   40

Evening Poem   42

Tithonus   45

And so he goes on   81

FALLING AWAKE

A SHORT STORY OF FALLING

It is the story of the falling rain
to turn into a leaf and fall again

it is the secret of a summer shower
to steal the light and hide it in a flower

and every flower a tiny tributary
that from the ground flows green and momentary

is one of water's wishes and this tale
hangs in a seed-head smaller than my thumbnail

if only I a passerby could pass
as clear as water through a plume of grass

to find the sunlight hidden at the tip
turning to seed a kind of lifting rain drip

then I might know like water how to balance
the weight of hope against the light of patience

water which is so raw so earthy-strong
and lurks in cast-iron tanks and leaks along

drawn under gravity towards my tongue
to cool and fill the pipe-work of this song

which is the story of the falling rain
that rises to the light and falls again

SWAN

A rotted swan
is hurrying away from the plane-crash mess of her wings
                    one here
                            one there

getting panicky up out of her clothes and mid-splash
    looking down again at what a horrible plastic
mould of herself split-second
climbing out of her own cockpit

and lifting away again and bending back for another look thinking
                    strange
                            strange
what are those two white clips that connected my strength
    to its floatings

and lifting away again and bending back for another look
at the clean china serving-dish of a breast bone
and how thickly the symmetrical quill-points
were threaded in backwards through the leather underdress
    of the heart saying

                    strange
                            strange
it's not as if such fastenings could ever contain
the regular yearning wing-beat of my evenings
and that surely can't be my own black feet
lying poised in their slippers

what a waste of detail
what a heaviness inside each feather

and leaving her life and all its tools
with their rusty juices trickling back to the river
she is lifting away she is taking a last look thinking

      quick

            quick

            say something to the
            frozen cloud of the head
            before it thaws

            whose one dead eye
            is a growing cone of twilight
            in the middle of winter

            it is snowing there
            and the bride has just set out
            to walk to her wedding

            but how can she reach
            the little black-lit church
            it is so cold

            the bells like iron angels
            hung from one note
            keep ringing and ringing

FLIES

This is the day the flies fall awake mid-sentence
and lie stunned on the window-sill shaking with speeches
only it isn't speech it is trembling sections of puzzlement which
break off suddenly as if the questioner had been shot

this is one of those wordy days
when they drop from their winter quarters in the curtains
    and sizzle as they fall
feeling like old cigarette butts called back to life
blown from the surface of some charred world

and somehow their wings which are little more than flakes
    of dead skin
have carried them to this blackened disembodied question

what dirt shall we visit today?
what dirt shall we re-visit?

they lift their faces to the past and walk about a bit
trying out their broken thought-machines
coming back with their used-up words

there is such a horrible trapped buzzing wherever we fly
it's going to be impossible to think clearly now until next winter
what should we
what dirt should we

FOX

I heard a cough
as if a thief was there
outside my sleep
a sharp intake of air

a fox in her fox-fur
stepping across
the grass in her black gloves
barked at my house

just so abrupt and odd
the way she went
hungrily asking
in the heart's thick accent

in such serious sleepless
trespass she came
a woman with a man's voice
but no name

as if to say: it's midnight
and my life
is laid beneath my children
like gold leaf

SEVERED HEAD FLOATING DOWNRIVER

It is said that after losing his wife, Orpheus was torn to pieces by Maenads, who threw his head into the River Hebron. The head went on singing and forgetting, filling up with water and floating away.

Eurydice   already forgetting who she is
with her shoes missing
and the grass coming up through her feet

searching the earth
          for the bracelet of tiny weave on her charcoal wrist

the name of a fly or flower   already forgetting who they are
they grow they grow
         till their bodies break their necks

down there in the stone world
where the grey spirits of stones lie around uncertain of their limits
matter is eating my mind   I am in a river

            I in my fox-cap
floating between the speechless reeds
I always wake like this being watched

already forgetting who I am
the water wears my mask   I call   I call
lying under its lashes like a glance

if only a child on a bridge would hoik me out

there comes a tremor and there comes a pause

down there in the underworld
where the tired stones have fallen
and the sand in a trance lifts a little
                    it is always midnight in those pools

iron insects engraved in sleep

                    I always wake like this being watched

I always speak to myself
                    no more myself but a colander
draining the sound from this never-to-be-mentioned wound

can you hear it
you with your long shadows and your short shadows

can you hear the severed head of Orpheus

no I feel nothing from the neck down

already forgetting who I am
the crime goes on without volition singing in its bone
                not I not I
                        the water drinks my mind

as if in a black suit
                as if bent to my books
                only my face exists sliding over a waterfall

and there where the ferns hang over the dark
and the midges move between mirrors
some woman has left her shoes
                              two crumpled mouths
            which my voice searches in and out

my voice being water
which holds me together and also carries me away
until the facts forget themselves gradually like a contrail

and all this week
            a lime-green light troubles the riverbed
            as if the mud was haunted by the wood

this is how the wind works hard at thinking
this is what speaks when no one speaks

COLD STREAK

I notice a cold streak
I notice it in the sun
all that dazzling stubbornness
of keeping to its clock

I notice the fatigue of flowers
weighed down by light
I notice the lark has a needle
pulled through its throat

why don't they put down their instruments?
I notice they never pause
I notice the dark sediment of their singing
covers the moors like soot blown under a doorway

almost everything here has cold hands
I notice the wind wears surgical gloves
I notice the keen pale colours of the rain
like a surgeon's assistant

why don't they lift their weight
and see what's flattened underneath it?
I notice the thin meticulous grass,
thrives in this place

BODY

This is what happened
the dead were settling in under their mud roof
and something was shuffling overhead

it was a badger treading on the thin partition

bewildered were the dead
going about their days and nights in the dark
putting their feet down carefully and finding themselves floating
but that badger

still with the simple heavy box of his body needing to be lifted
was shuffling away alive

hard at work
with the living shovel of himself
into the lane he dropped
        not once looking up

and missed the sight of his own corpse falling like a suitcase
    towards him
with the grin like an opened zip
        (as I found it this morning)

and went on running with that bindweed will of his
went on running along the hedge and into the earth again
trembling
as if in a broken jug for one backwards moment
            water might keep its shape

A RUSHED ACCOUNT OF THE DEW

I who can blink
to break the spell of daylight

and what a sliding screen between worlds
is a blink

I who can hear the last three seconds in my head
but the present is beyond me
               listen

in this tiny moment of reflexion
I want to work out what it's like to descend
out of the dawn's mind

and find a leaf and fasten the known to the unknown
with a liquid cufflink
               and then unfasten

to be brief

to be almost actual

oh pristine example
of claiming a place on the earth
only to cancel

SHADOW

I'm going to flicker for a moment
and tell you the tale of a shadow
    that falls at dusk
        out of the blue to the earth
        and turns left along the path to here

        groggily under its black-out
        being dragged along crippled over things as if broken-winged

not yet continuous
no more than a shiver of something
with the flesh parachute of a human opening above it

but lengthening a little as it descends through the rings
of one hour into the next

        with the rooks flying upwards snipping at the clouds

until at last out of that opening here it lies
my own impersonal pronoun
crumpled under me like a dead body

it is faint
it has been falling for a long time

look when I walk
it's like a pair of scissors thrown at me by the sun
so that now as if my skin were not quite tucked in
    I am cold cold
trying to slide myself out of my own shade
but hour by hour more shade leaks out

    or if I stand
        if I move one hand
    I hear the hiss of flowers closing their eyelids
    and the trees
as if dust was being beaten from a rug
        shake out their birds and in again

it's as if I've interrupted something
that was falling in a straight line from the eye of God

    and if I do nothing
    the ground gives up
    the almost minty clarity of its grass begins to fade
    the white moths under the leaves
        are amazed

VILLAGE

Somebody out late again say what you like
sinister walk throwing one foot forward
black jumble-sale clothes with a bit of string around the knees
going over the mud with a tread like that throwing one foot forward

somebody out not back being out again
walking every evening as regular as the rooks
throwing one foot forward so many names in this place are you listening
taking his bucket to the tap

John Strong

that's him bursting full of himself hook-nosed sinister walk
scars on each side of the wrist no teeth
not known for his beauty having been shot in the mouth
black jumble-sale clothes

[...]

somebody out thankfully not me out lost in the mud
somebody lost out late again say what you like
a boot by the granite trough not many of us left
living in the slippery maybe the last green places are you listening

not many of us left not much movement
in the blackening lanes among a few low trees
little flocks of orchids in the ditches nobody cares
it's as dark as a pond down here we could do with a hedge-flail

with a scythe somebody with a scythe
you can hear him smashing through six-foot nettles
black jumble-sale clothes with a bit of string around the knees
so as the rats won't run up his legs are you listening

Thomas Lytch

that's him in the rain now
somebody with a tread like that
very chilblain slow with a lump on his toe
just saw him on the way back home again mud in his mouth

[...]

I said the dirt gets right into your fingers
living under the trees like this the toads don't mind it
this is god's honest truth there's one about as big as a bucket
hops out of the nettles every night you can say what you like

that's him slugging about the village bent-headed
heavily laden with the cold you can tell it's him
spillikin legs always wet for some reason
always poking the verges looking for a tasty bit of nothing

always wet for some reason always standing like a bale in the rain
remembering better times whereas naming no names
some of us would rather not remember something
some of us have got enough bloody nightmares already

somebody a bundle of nerves ever since the wall came down
won't barely go out of the church now
ever since a bat swooped in like a pair of leather gloves feeling her face
had to dive under the pews for cover this is god's honest truth

Joyce Jones

just heard her voice again say what you like
cold nights without streetlights
walking to the sea perhaps
on the soft of her feet with a stout stick why

[...]

somebody out peering out not me
red face at the window regular every evening
not noted for his warmth this is god's honest truth
not noted for his warmth no wife

somebody out late talking in the street
not many of us left no shop long weeds in the hedges
it's as dull as a pond down here what a hiss in the throat
having been gassed in the war that voice is are you listening

is that somebody's bed-ridden red face peering out
won't barely go out of the house now is that smoke
are they burning the trees again say what you like
she won't like that not many of us left

so many names in this place not many of us left
living on the last we can find can you hear this
somebody out peering out not me noticed the least likely
    the very soul of respectability
eating something in the cemetery not rats I hope are you listening

listen somebody's sister the very soul of respectability
without one word of a lie just this very morning
being in her slippers having recently put out the trash
had the misfortune to die over the dustbins in the snow

Lyn Waters

of course somebody had to shift her say what you like
just saw him with a grim look
put her in the car boot cold as a trout
with a bit of green silk around the middle to protect against rheumatism

[...]

somebody as barely there as light as a lace curtain
lying in the nettles with her teeth upwards
couldn't lift herself
been living off nettles for a week hence the expression

somebody on her knees again not what she was
somebody screaming again last night being strangled or something
good grief you get used to the sounds not many of us left
living on the fluff of green of the last little floes of the earth

VERTIGO

May I shuffle forward and tell you the two-minute life of rain
starting right now lips open and lidless-cold all-seeing gaze

when something not yet anything changes its mind like me
and begins to fall
           in the small hours

and the light is still a flying carpet
only a little white between worlds like an eye opening
     after an operation

no turning back
           each drop is a snap decision
a suicide from the tower-block of heaven

and for the next ten seconds
the rain stares at the ground

sees me stirring here
as if sculpted in porridge

sees the garden in the green of its mind already drinking
and the grass lengthening

           stalls

maybe a thousand feet above me
a kind of yellowness or levity
like those tiny alterations that brush the legs of swimmers
lifts the rain a little to the left

no more than a flash of free-will
until the clouds close their options and the whole

    melancholy air
        surrenders to pure fear and
           falls

and I who live in the basement
one level down from the world
with my eyes to the insects with my ears to the roots
                listening

I feel them in my bones these dead straight lines
coming closer and closer to my core

this is the sound this is the very floor
where Grief and his Wife are living
         looking up

LOOKING DOWN

Clouds: I can watch their films in puddles
passionate and slow without obligations of shape or stillness

I can stand with wilted neck and look
                              directly into the drowned corpse of a cloud

it is cold-blooded down there
precisely outlined as if under a spell
                              and it narrows to a weighted point which
                              throws back darkness

oh yes there is a trembling rod that hangs my head above puddles
and the clouds like trapped smoke wander under me
and the sun lies discarded on the tarmac
                                        like an old
                        white
            shoe

        don't go on about those other clouds
        those high pre-historic space-ferns
        that steam the windows of the wind
        I know I could look up and see them
                    curled like fossils in the troposphere

but I am here

I have been leaning here a long time hunched
under the bone lintel of my stare

with the whole sky
                    dropped and rippling through my eye
and now a crow on a glass lens
slides through the earth

ALONGSIDE BEANS

Weeding alongside beans in the same rush as them

6 a.m. scrabbling at the earth

beans synchronised in rows
soft fanatical irresponsible beans
behind my back
breaking out of their mass grave

at first, just a rolled-up flag
then a bayonet a pair of gloved hands

then a shocked corpse hurrying up in prayer
and then another

and then (as if a lock had gone and the Spring had broken loose)
        a hoverfly

not looking up but lost in pause
        landing its full-stop
on a bean leaf

(and what a stomach bursting from its straps
what a nervous readiness attached to its lament and
using the sound as a guard rail over the drop)

and then another

and after a while a flower
turning its head to the side like a bored emperor

and after a while a flower

singing out a faint line of scent
and spinning around the same obsession with its task
and working with the same bewitched slightly off-hand look
    as the sea

        covering first one place

and then another

and after a while another place

        and then another place

            and another

                and another

A DRINK FROM CRANMERE POOL

Amphibious vagueness
neither pool nor land
under whose velvet
three rivers spring to their tasks

in whose indecent hills
tired of my voice
I followed the advice of water
knelt and put my mouth

to a socket in the grass
as if to an outlet of my own
unveiled stoneliness
and sleepless flight

they say the herons used to hang
like lamps here giving off gloom
now walkers float
on the wings of their macs

to this weephole
where you can taste
almost
not water exactly

SLOWED-DOWN BLACKBIRD

Three people in the snow
getting rid of themselves
        breath by breath

and every six seconds a blackbird

three people in raincoats losing their tracks in the snow
walking as far as the edge and back again
with the trees exhausted
        tapping at the sky

and every six seconds a blackbird

first three then two
passing one eye between them
and the eye is a white eraser rubbing them away

and on the edge a blackbird
trying over and over its broken line
trying over and over its broken line

DUNT: A POEM FOR A DRIED-UP RIVER

Very small and damaged and quite dry,
a Roman water nymph made of bone
tries to summon a river out of limestone

very eroded faded
her left arm missing and both legs from the knee down
a Roman water nymph made of bone
tries to summon a river out of limestone

exhausted   utterly worn down
a Roman water nymph made of bone
being the last known speaker of her language
she tries to summon a river out of limestone

little distant sound of dry grass   try again

a Roman water nymph made of bone
very endangered now
in a largely unintelligible monotone
she tries to summon a river out of limestone

little distant sound as of dry grass   try again

exquisite bone figurine with upturned urn
in her passionate self-esteem she smiles looking sideways
she seemingly has no voice but a throat-clearing rustle
as of dry grass   try again

she tries leaning
pouring pure outwardness out of a grey urn

little slithering sounds as of a rabbit man in full night-gear,
who lies so low in the rickety willowherb
that a fox trots out of the woods
and over his back and away   try again

she tries leaning
pouring pure outwardness out of a grey urn
little lapping sounds   yes
as of dry grass secretly drinking   try again

little lapping sounds   yes
as of dry grass secretly drinking   try again

Roman bone figurine

year after year in a sealed glass case

having lost the hearing of her surroundings

she struggles to summon a river out of limestone

little shuffling sound as of approaching slippers

year after year in a sealed glass case

a Roman water nymph made of bone

she struggles to summon a river out of limestone

little shuffling sound as of a nearly dried-up woman

not really moving through the fields

having had the gleam taken out of her

to the point where she resembles twilight   try again

little shuffling clicking

she opens the door of the church

little distant sounds of shut-away singing   try again

little whispering fidgeting of a shut-away congregation

wondering who to pray to

little patter of eyes closing   try again

very small and damaged and quite dry
a Roman water nymph made of bone
she pleads she pleads a river out of limestone

little hobbling tripping of a nearly dried-up river
not really moving through the fields,
having had the gleam taken out of it
to the point where it resembles twilight.
little grumbling shivering last-ditch attempt at a river
more nettles than water   try again

very speechless very broken old woman
her left arm missing and both legs from the knee down
she tries to summon a river out of limestone

little stoved-in sucked thin
low-burning glint of stones
rough-sleeping and trembling and clinging to its rights
victim of Swindon
puddle midden
slum of over-greened foot-churn and pats
whose crayfish are cheap tool-kits
made of the mud stirred up when a stone's lifted

it's a pitiable likeness of clear running
struggling to keep up with what's already gone
the boat the wheel the sluice gate
the two otters larricking along   go on

and they say oh they say
in the days of better rainfall
it would flood through five valleys
there'd be cows and milking stools
washed over the garden walls
and when it froze you could skate for five miles   yes go on

little loose end shorthand unrepresented
beautiful disused route to the sea
fish path with nearly no fish in

TWO VOICES

I own the dawn! the cockerel claims. The light
still loiters with intent to take the night.
Wind steals through woods, the democratic dew
gives equal weight to everything. A few
blank seconds and he starts again. He yawns
and voice possesses him. I own all dawns!
I stand on dignity! he shouts out, shut
in the dark kingdom of his one-room flat.
More pained possessive crazed each time he crows
he has to wrench his larynx, curl his claws
to let that shout surge through him. Glancing out
I notice nothing answers except light,
whose answer makes the earth's hairs stand on end
and shadows fall full-length without a sound.

What is the word for wordless, when the ground
bursts into crickets? There's a creaking sound
like speaking speeded up. A skeleton
crawls across leaves, still in its cramped position.
one minute stooping on a bending blade
rubbing its painful elbows, next minute made
of pinged elastic, flying hypertense,
speaking in several languages at once.
not like a mouth might speak, more like two hands
make whispered contact through their finger-ends,
like light itself which absent-mindedly
brushes the grass and speaks by letting be,
but when you duck down suddenly and stare
into the startled stems, there's nothing there.

SUNDAY BALLAD

A questioner called Light appeared,
with probe and beam
began to search the room
where two lay twined in bed.

whose intellect surpassing theirs
with no regard
for things half-dressed
accused them of old age

as weak as eggs they woke.
they thought their bodies
gleaming in the window-square
felt less like age than air

oh no not quite
in blue pedantic Light
two doors away two trees
made less of leaves than sound

as if to prove them wrong
described the wind
and as they dressed the dust
flew white and silent through the house

YOU MUST NEVER SLEEP UNDER A MAGNOLIA

when the tree begins to flower
like a glimpse of

Flesh

when the flower begins to smell
as if its roots have reached

the layer of
Thirst upon the
unsealed jar of

Joy

Alice, you should
never sleep under
so much pure pale

so many shriek-mouthed blooms

as if Patience
had run out of

Patience

ASIDE

In Berkshire somewhere 1970
I hid in a laurel bush outside a house,
planted in gravel I think.
I stopped running and just pushed open
its oilskin flaps and settled down
in some kind of waiting room, whose scarred boughs
had clearly been leaning and kneeling there
for a long time. They were bright black.

I remember this Museum of Twilight
was low-ceilinged and hear-through
as through a bedroom window
one hears the zone of someone's afternoon
being shouted and shouted in, but by now
I was too evergreen to answer, watching
the woodlice at work in hard hats
taking their trolleys up and down.

through longer and longer interims
a dead leaf fell, rigidly yellow and slow.
so by degrees I became invisible
in that spotted sick-room light
and nobody found me there.
the hour has not yet ended in which
under a cloth of laurel
I sat quite still.

Sz

good morning to you, first faint breeze of unrest
no louder than the sound of the ear unzipping,
late-comer, mere punctuation between seasons
whom the Chinese call
Sz

forgive me, small-mouth,
I heard you criticise the earth
and stepped outside to see the fields ruffle your cloth,
but you were moving on:
monotonous
vindictive
dust-bearing
scrupulous
one of many mass-produced particles of time
by whom the fruit has small frost-marks
and their hearts are already eroded and I
too

if you think, leaf-thief,
if you think I care
about your soft-spoken
head-in-the-clouds
seizure of another and yet another and yet another hour

then hear me, Sz,
you are so bodiless, so barely there
that I can only see you through starlings
whom you try this way and that like an uncomfortable coat
and then abandon

EVENING POEM

Old scrap-iron foxgloves
rusty rods of the broken woods

what a faded knocked-out stiffness
as if you'd sprung from the horse-hair
          of a whole Victorian sofa buried in the mud down there

or at any rate something dropped from a great height
straight through flesh and out the other side
has left your casing pale and loose and finally

just a heap of shoes

they say the gods being so uplifted
can't really walk on feet but take tottering steps
and lean like this closer and closer to the ground

                    which gods?

it is the hours on bird-thin legs
the same old choirs of hours
returning their summer clothes to the earth

with the night now
as if dropped from a great height

falling

TITHONUS

46 MINUTES IN THE LIFE OF THE DAWN

It is said that the dawn fell in love with Tithonus and asked Zeus to make him immortal, but forgot to ask that he should not grow old. Unable to die, he grew older and older until at last the dawn locked him in a room where he still sits babbling to himself and waiting night after night for her appearance.

What you are about to hear is the sound of Tithonus meeting the dawn at midsummer. His voice starts at 4.17, when the sun is six degrees below the horizon, and stops 46 minutes later, at sunrise. The performance will begin in darkness.

as soon as dawn appears

as soon as dawn appears

4:17 dressed only in her clouds

     and murk hangs down over hills
as if guilty

     two rooks quite high above steel
blue still a star
     and something similar to laughter
moves up from below making ducks
distracted

     two sounds you can hear at this
tucked-up hour
     when a man rolls over and pulls
his grief to his chin and his feet have
no covers
     first this: the sound of everything
repeating

then this: the sound of everything
repeating

as soon as dawn appears and the
river without interfering steals into
the morning
    bleak shapes of the last efforts of
the night
    and half-formed faces float out
and vanish too undulating to be
actual

as soon as a voice goes on arguing
in its sleep like a file going to and
corrosively fro
    doesn't sound like a man sounds
more like an instrument's voice very
small
    so the thought goes on recycling
itself and the mouth opens and the
body begins to shrivel into some-
thing more portable
    which is me old unfinished not
yet gone here I go again

as soon as a hand whose hand as
soon as the fingers feel for the clock

    4:22 the village is lost in its veils
a few dreams lean over the lanes like
nettles
    here come cascades of earliness in
which everything is asked is it light
is it light is it light
    the horizon making only muffled
answers but moisture on leaves is
quick to throw glances
    and bodiless black lace woods in
which one to another a songbird asks
    is it light is it light

not quite

as soon as the half moon looks
lost for words

as soon as an old man frozen on
his way to bed begins to melt and
smudges his nose-drip
and cautiously puts his hand
between his ribs and feels something
wet and sweet like stewed apple this
must be the heart this is only a dream

when a man rolls over and sighs

very nearly anonymous now
having recently turned five thousand
with the same wedge of yearning
lodged in my chest as ever
and getting accustomed to
surviving like a bramble very good
at growing anywhere you ought to
praise me for this trailing bloom this
must be the heart this is only a dream

when a man rolls over and sighs

very nearly anonymous now
having recently turned five
thousand with the same wedge of
yearning lodged in my chest as ever
    and getting accustomed to
surviving like a bramble very good
at growing anywhere
    and hearing myself churring and
wheezing
    and hearing myself through a
chink in my head examining the
whole horizonless question of desire
this must be the heart this must be
my innermost thought this is only
a dream

when a man rolls over and sighs

yes night after night he lies
enamelled by the whitening sky
    and first the damp and then the
dawn appear
    which hold him here so hunger-
eyed he can't quite

    die

    and so his mouth on grey wings
ascends being sucked away

    as soon as old thin and bone
did you ever hear such an insult
    jumps up amorous and cracking
his joints with excitement goes on
goes on babbling to himself
    draped to the chin in a dust-sheet
like a ghost's napkin and takes his
teaspoon of meat-juice

which is me again old
leaky-mouth eternal evening leaning
towards morning but she as if too
live to last defers her closeness

only a smirk of mauve on a
cloud's edge

it's 4:25 I thought I heard myself
being looked for what is it I said
what is it madam that you wish to
imply

she lets four seedheads show up
knotted against mud in hard exacting
detail
she never quite completes her
sentence but is always almost

and this is what draws me to the
window this huge fragment broken
off with the mind-spire winding
through it also unfinished

Music

she never quite completes her
sentence but is always almost
and this is what draws me to the
window too late I notice my head
still balanced on my neck but severed
by light from myself not knowing
but almost

what a non-sequitur from a seagull
at the height of falling

as soon as one rook too black goes
into smoky trees saying nothing and
the wood still lost in its inmost
unable
and mist forms an orderly queue
for the horizon

green ropes of wind white silks
of field
    and buried under several feet of
colour the eyes can never quite see
out but it is glittering now in the
gaps between things
    and the thistle begins to be
properly named and certain of its
spikes
    what a chandelier of dock flowers
dangles from the ground inverted
    so the morning and I meet up
again but not on talking terms

Music

    now a snail the speechless tongue
of one who is introverted and clings
to leaves
    pokes out of sleep too feelingly
as if a heart had been tinned and
opened

now laughing mallards pull
themselves together
　　now swans make straight lines
across water

　　now webs on twigs now the rapid
whisper of a grasshopper scraping
back and forth as if working at rust

　　and now a gorse bush as I glance
towards it a sort of swelling yellow-
ness a smelling somehowness
　　barely keeps still enough to be
certain
　　while a fern unfolds growing
outside the time zone

now 4:32 now 4:33

now a lark in a prayer-draught
shakes the air
    and the hour is quickened by
crows with their rusty voice-handles
    and pre-world owls too impartial
to be swayed
    and ear-splitting over-actual
blackbirds
    and magpies coming straight
from a meeting with misfortune

    oh the whistles in the bushes
have never heard of evenings
    and new-born tunes know nothing
of my thick-skinned listening
    now being washed by a single
thrush

    rewinding and grieving

    rewinding and grieving

and now the first wood doves
start up litigations in the trees
    I can't help thinking of birds'
heads thrust forwards it makes
excitements even to say so
    slow-motion puffs of mood
getting ready to ascend with drapery
lifted and tiny dandruff weed-flowers

    there is amazement here turning
wishfully pink above trees and two
sharp slices of seagull weird squawks
of night-thoughts trying to dream
again
    so the voice stumbles and the feet
can't get comfortable and the eyes
flicker under so much
    peach-pale air apparently peering
down and hurrying away and
peering down and hurrying
backwards away

who could be close to so much
cold inspection
    it makes me shiver like a dead
soldier returning his empty clothes
to his bride but she's married
someone else
    so the eyes stare and the hands
lifted to feel her there curl up like
crumpled leaves and fall back to the
ground

    as soon as the whole sky is laid out
long and beginning and muted with
damp in a colour of descended hope
    and hearing the lurch the
well-known slap of joy when
bird-verse takes a regular line and
the wood is now graffitied on a pale
wall
    and a great proximity arches
overhead

    mother of the winds I can't speak
this half-descript unable to unblend
itself from things
    nothing yet has a shadow every-
thing is here but pale tell me madam
why so encrypted
    and what precisely is this shining

    stuff

    it's just a cloth they answer
speaking that rustling speech I
always hear it in the grass a bit like
sound being reduced to sand
    the sky's a cloth the eye a passer-
by with mirrors
    behind that cloth another cloth
behind that cloth another cloth and
then another cloth and then another

Music

Etc.

willows I want to pause and praise
you who used to be headstrong and
have now forgiven everything
    growing lenient and bowed as I am

    grasses I'm going to speak your
names
    like a traveller staring through a
newspaper mouthing the headlines
    and the page whispers as he reads

    and then another thing and then
another
    and then another thing and then
another

as for the sparrows I've been
watching them embroider their
indecisions in brown stitches until
the whole valley is darned
   then leaving their dusty jackets on
the ground
   and then another life and then
another

   and then a chaffinch starts and
then another

   then self-made moss then midges
whose whole surface is a sound-wave

then something the same in every
hedge doesn't speak like a speech
    more like an inkling like a ticking
like an inner working turning this
way and that

    you should see the beetle's fingers
feeling forwards for the levers of the
earth
    they begin to chafe they begin to
click they begin to blur they begin to
braille

    and my voice then speaks with
spaces much as a sewing machine
might write with no thread a line
of small holes

and then another thing and then
another

and then a chaffinch starts and
then another

and starts and starts

and then a chaffinch starts with a
long run-up to reach the same old
execration
and a spider looking neither left
nor right with the same obsessive
unbalanced
then midges the same then
bindweed still in her white night
clothes in the same long entangle-
ment slightly sticky to the touch

the same dizziness the same life
like a metal beam whacks me on the
head again as when a man slinks
home after battle
alive alive and nobody else was
that lucky
who is it trapped in this living
shape pushing the door with his
hands still covered in blood
and makes some toast and leans
like a fold-up stool against the wall
and there he still sits the next
morning

4.49 with the same old grief as
mine is it mine am I home oh how
much life not my own have I
buttered and eaten

as soon as the grief as soon as a
ghost begins to shake me from the
inside

as soon as my hair which roots in
the very top of the mind where the
dead have floated
    comes out of crevices unbranched
and produces long stems without
flowers

as soon as an old man runs his
finger along his gums and thinks of
his teeth
one or two have gone missing
from the little collection left lying
in the mouth
if only they had been cleaned
and kept in their box

this broken yellow bracelet was
once a smile the priceless gift of the
family very useful for meetings

what meetings seeing as the very
moment is itself a movement

Music

so flies dispute precise points
the definitions are written
    a kiss gives off a swoosh of
amnesia or is it moths letting the
mood pass through their feelers
and out the other side

    when a man dries up and rolls
on the ground still speaking
    as if brushing away the shock
of the dawn

    which is a wall of green

    which is a small field sliding at the
speed of light straight through the
house and on to the surface of the
eye

which is love's property

which is light's equal

which is a beam of dust

which is the classical or fluted
style of coming in through curtains

which is a memory

which happens again and again

every morning the same repeti-
tion spreads its infection a kiss gives
off a swoosh

which is one of light's moods

which is exhausted

which is waves of forms and folds
being added to leaves

and the humorous angular manner
of claiming instantly whatever
surface is offered

which is mine

the survivor

the makeshift character that
springs from speaking and looking
on and letting everything pass and
then the loneliness of being left here
endless lost to my lethargy like a
dripping tap

but what a ballast of abdomen
what a block of hope what a
kleptomaniac what a thief of life

I am

Music

as soon as dawn one star then
suddenly none then blue then pale
and the whole apparition only
ever known backwards already too
late now almost gone

as soon as orange crimson gold

as soon as each tree becomes
particular and a working wood
emerges and the river begins to speak
back with underwater woodland

as soon as the light the first awake
as soon as earliness calling softly to
the trees to be unsettled please
    she whoever she is who gropes for
the mind and rips it open as soon as
that goddess unconcealed
    with the same unspoken sound as
dew consents to the ground
    and little shadows hurry
undecidedly aside quick quick in
these final moments of closeness

then at last whatever it is

5.03 as the sun saws the morning
into beams

with splintered eyes and incessant
insect murmur of a man praying and
rubbing his legs and hissing through
a crack in his flesh-boards

asks

may I stop please

And so he goes on dwindling away
maybe through too much prayer
is now too rarefied to touch
or settle anywhere

and falls to whispering here
as lost as dust
in darklight under grass
in chorus with unanimous unrest

whose hearsays half-thoughts
twinkling on and off
I never quite make out
or not

what is the word for something
fashioned in the quick of hearing
but never quite
but never quite
                    appearing

Poems in this collection have previously been published by or in association with: *Agni*, Bernard Jacobson Gallery, Bristol Lyrical Ballads Project, Desperate Men (for Battle of the Winds), Graywolf Press, *Guardian*, Kew Bridge West Design Development, The Letter Press, *Literary Review*, London Literature Festival | Southbank Centre, The Poetry Society, Royal Collection Trust, Royal Society of Arts, *Spectator*.

Thanks to: Robin Robertson, Jill Bialosky, Kevin Mount, Peter Oswald, Jane Borodale, Paul Keegan, Jeff Shotts, Laurence Green, Laura Beatty and the Keens, Griselda Sanderson, James Runcie, Joe Richards, Tony Merrit, Mark Payne, Luke Parker.